Set design by Anita Stewart *Photo by Darren Setlow*

Alexis Camins in a scene from the Portland Stage Company production of *Yemaya's Belly*.

YEMAYA'S BELLY

BY QUIARA ALEGRÍA HUDES

DRAMATISTS
PLAY SERVICE
INC.

YEMAYA'S BELLY
Copyright © 2007, Quiara Alegría Hudes

All Rights Reserved

CAUTION: Professionals and amateurs are hereby warned that performance of YEMAYA'S BELLY is subject to payment of a royalty. It is fully protected under the copyright laws of the United States of America, and of all countries covered by the International Copyright Union (including the Dominion of Canada and the rest of the British Commonwealth), and of all countries covered by the Pan-American Copyright Convention, the Universal Copyright Convention, the Berne Convention, and of all countries with which the United States has reciprocal copyright relations. All rights, including without limitation professional/amateur stage rights, motion picture, recitation, lecturing, public reading, radio broadcasting, television, video or sound recording, all other forms of mechanical, electronic and digital reproduction, transmission and distribution, such as CD, DVD, the Internet, private and file-sharing networks, information storage and retrieval systems, photocopying, and the rights of translation into foreign languages are strictly reserved. Particular emphasis is placed upon the matter of readings, permission for which must be secured from the Author's agent in writing.

The English language stock and amateur stage performance rights in the United States, its territories, possessions and Canada for YEMAYA'S BELLY are controlled exclusively by DRAMATISTS PLAY SERVICE, INC., 440 Park Avenue South, New York, NY 10016. No professional or nonprofessional performance of the Play may be given without obtaining in advance the written permission of DRAMATISTS PLAY SERVICE, INC., and paying the requisite fee.

Inquiries concerning all other rights should be addressed to Bret Adams Ltd., 448 West 44th Street, New York, NY 10036. Attn: Bruce Ostler.

SPECIAL NOTE

Anyone receiving permission to produce YEMAYA'S BELLY is required to give credit to the Author as sole and exclusive Author of the Play on the title page of all programs distributed in connection with performances of the Play and in all instances in which the title of the Play appears for purposes of advertising, publicizing or otherwise exploiting the Play and/or a production thereof. The name of the Author must appear on a separate line, in which no other name appears, immediately beneath the title and in size of type equal to 50% of the size of the largest, most prominent letter used for the title of the Play. No person, firm or entity may receive credit larger or more prominent than that accorded the Author. The following acknowledgment must appear on the title page in all programs distributed in connection with performances of the Play:

Professional Premiere Production
Portland Stage Company
Anita Stewart, Artistic Director
Tamera Ramaker, Managing Director

For Sedo.

Special thanks to Ray, Paula, and Mom.

An early version of YEMAYA'S BELLY was produced by Miracle Theatre (Olga Sanchez, Artistic Director) in February, 2004. It was directed by Sacha Reich.

YEMAYA'S BELLY was premiered by Portland Stage Company (Anita Stewart, Artistic Director; Tamera Ramaker, Managing Director) in Portland, Maine, on March 1, 2005. It was directed by Peter Sampieri; the set design was by Anita Stewart; the lighting design was by Bryon Winn; and the music was composed and performed live by Shamou. The cast was as follows:

JESUS/MULO	Alexis Camins
YEMAYA/MAYA	Stephanie Beatriz
JELIN	Joaquin Torres
TICO	Gilbert Cruz
LILA/MAMI	Brigitte Viellieu-Davis

CHARACTERS

JESUS/MULO — a boy, 12 (hay-soos, moo-lo)
JELIN — Jesus' uncle (hay-leen)
TICO — a man who hacks open coconuts (tee-ko)
LILA — owner of a grocery store
& MAMI — Jesus' mother
MAYA — a girl on a boat
& YEMAYA — a young festival performer

SETTING

Recent history.

The ocean. It may be miles away, a distant whisper. Or we may be underwater. We are always in relation to the ocean. A thousand shades of blue moving in waves. Sometimes the motion is soothing. Other times it is violent. The wind influences the ocean.

Real items float to the surface. Dominoes. A duck feather. A Coke bottle. A coconut husk. Rice. Shovels. A machete. Things that tell us where we are.

RITUALS

Some actions are designated as rituals:

(Ritual: Jesus holds the bottle of Coke in one hand. When the cold starts to burn, he switches the bottle to the other hand and shakes out the burning hand for relief ... End ritual.)

A ritual involves a body and an object, together in a moment of possession. Rituals are crude, physically exaggerated. They make the body raw.

PRODUCTION NOTE: Though the text seems poetic, and the rituals give a sense of magic realism, it is imperative that these characters and their situations be as real and as specific as possible. Be wary of making the play overly magical. The moments of poetry should be surprises, should stand out against a starker, more impoverished landscape. These characters are hungry; they do not have a lot. Also, please research Yemaya specifically and respectfully. Do not treat her presence as generic multi-cultural myth or fantasy, but as a specific cultural phenomenon that should be respected.

And what if someone said:
"Be careful of the ocean deeps:
Or its depths will be your gravestone"
Would it be wise to take a boat
And set out from harbour in the middle of a storm?
—Calderon, *Life Is a Dream*

YEMAYA'S BELLY

SCENE 1

A mountain farming town on an island. It is accessible by one narrow road that winds up the side of the mountain. Just when it seems the road couldn't possibly go any higher, there is Magdalena. Sunrise on a mountaintop farm. The wind blows ferociously. Jesus and Mami are on their farm.

MAMI. Jesus! Bring your father his cup of coffee.
JESUS. I already brought him one.
MAMI. Grownups need at least two cups.
JESUS. He's being a grouch. I asked him why it's so windy and he said to leave him in peace.
MAMI. It's windy because St. Peter opened up the gates of heaven to let someone in.
JESUS. They must be some huge gates.
MAMI. Be careful with the wind. Don't spill it. *(She hands him the cup and leaves. The wind blows in circles and spirals.)*
JESUS.
    Red white and blue
    Sugar and gin
    My story begins
    Once there was a boy. It was Sunday and church was over. The boy wanted to buy a cookie so he asked his papi for a penny. "Oh, papi ... " But before the boy could finish his papi yelled, "No!" The boy said, "But papi ... " And the papi yelled, "No!" So the boy turned away and whispered, "Stiiingy." "Repeat it louder, so I can hear," the papi said. So the boy repeated it. "Stiiiiingy." And then the boy heard a growl come from inside the papi's belly. It sounded like the beginning of a hurricane. The boy took off running so the papi wouldn't smack him with the belt. He ran all the way to the top of

the coconut tree. And he spent the night up there and he didn't come down for dinner, even though his mami had made pork chops. That night, the wind was so strong that he flew away. *(He spreads his arms to fly. The coffee spills to the ground.)* He flew over the farm. He flew over the mountain. He flew over the ocean. He flew all the way to America, and he landed in the house of the President of America. He told the story about his stingy papi, and the President of America gave the boy a penny to buy a sugar cookie.

    Red white and blue
    Sugar and rum
    My story is done

MAMI. *(Yelling from the distance.)* Jesus! What are you doing? By the time you get there it's going to be cold.
JESUS. *(Realizing he spilled the coffee.)* Um … Papi said he didn't want any more coffee. But he said thank you anyway.
MAMI. Go and get ready for school. Your slacks and shirt are on the table.
JESUS. Can I have a penny for a cookie after school?
MAMI. And you better comb that hair. *(The wind blows in Jesus' face.)*

SCENE 2

Tico's bar stand at the roadside. An old produce crate is enjoying a second life as a retail counter. On the counter are some bottles of rum, a pile of coconuts with the green husk still on, and a machete to hack open the coconuts. Behind the crate sits Tico, an old dude. Jesus is at the counter.

JESUS. I'm broke. Papi wouldn't give me a penny.
TICO. If you want to do a job for me, you can earn a drink.
JESUS. Okay.
TICO. You're going to do my inventory. When you own a business, you always keep track of how much stuff you have. That's your inventory. It's a list. You say the item first, then how many you have.
JESUS. Coconuts, six. Bottles of rum, two. Beer, four. Straws, three. Machete, one.

TICO. That's it. A full day's work.
JESUS. What else is there to do?
TICO. You sit and wait for someone to come along. You just earned yourself a coconut. *(He demonstrates a coconut.)*
JESUS. Can I open it?
TICO. No. That's a job for experienced men only.
JESUS. How do you get experience?
TICO. Your father teaches you how to do it.
JESUS. Papi doesn't like to show me things.
TICO. Let me see you make a muscle. *(Jesus does. There's no muscle.)* This machete is heavy.
JESUS. I'm strong.
TICO. If you swing it the wrong way, there goes your pinky. Hold the coconut down with one hand. Swing the blade back and forth like this. Concentrate. You want to be precise. *(He demonstrates a smooth hacking motion. Jesus tries this. He hacks at the coconut chaotically and works up quite a sweat.)* It's not a pork chop. You don't nibble at it. You give it a good cut. *(Jesus tries using more force.)* Careful! You'll cut off your hand and the damn thing still won't be open. Watch how I do it. *(Tico takes the coconut. In four precise strokes through the air, he creates a hole in the top. He slips a drinking straw into the hole and gives it to Jesus.)* It takes practice before you get good. *(Jelin enters and plops down into one of the chairs. He punches Jesus' arm and ruffles his hair.)*
JELIN. Hey! Little Jesus! Shouldn't you be in school? You always want to be where the action is, don't you? Always hanging around with the big boys. You'll learn more from us anyway. What do they got to teach you in school that we don't already know? *(To Tico.)* Did the bus come through yet?
TICO. You got plenty of time. That thing always comes late.
JELIN. I'm heading down to the city. Take care of some business.
JESUS. Have you ever been in the city before?
JELIN. What do you think?
JESUS. What's it like?
JELIN. *(To Tico.)* So I heard you got in some trouble this weekend.
JESUS. Grownups can't get in trouble.
JELIN. *(To Jesus.)* Shh.
TICO. It's those damn Pentecostals. Baldomera is always dragging me to her Pentecostal meetings over at her brother's farm. You should see them. Out on the hill, singing and clapping. Speaking in tongues. So this weekend it's raining and thundering. Mud everywhere. She still makes me go. Everyone there is wet head to

toe, praying like fools. When we arrive at the meeting, hwa! I slip in some mud and land flat on my ass. Right in the middle of everybody. I yell out at the top of my lungs, "goddamn it!"

JESUS. You're not supposed to say that.

TICO. *(Silence.)* Everyone stops in their tracks and turns around and stares at me like I'm the devil. They said I'm never allowed back to another meeting.

JELIN. A happy ending! Why don't you pull out those dominoes?

TICO. I don't have anything to bet. *(Jelin hands Tico a couple bucks.)*

JELIN. You still owe me from last time. *(Jelin sets up the dominoes.)*

JESUS. I'm in.

JELIN. You got any money to put on the table?

JESUS. No, because my papi's stingy.

TICO. Let the kid play. He doesn't have to put any money down. *(To Jesus.)* Make up a bet.

JESUS. If I win, I go to the city with my uncle.

JELIN. Oh no. I'm going for grown-up stuff.

JESUS. I'll be good.

JELIN. Your father wouldn't approve. You know how he is.

JESUS. He's working. He won't find out.

JELIN. What do I care? It's not like the kid is going to beat me at dominoes.

TICO. I've been giving him lessons.

JELIN. All bets are on the table. *(Their domino game begins. It should be choreographed like a macho ballet. Shuffling: Jelin pours the dominoes on the table and swirls them around. They make clicking sounds as they are shuffled. He deals each player their pieces. Jelin moves: He slides the domino on a teasing, curvy path along the table. Just before playing it, he lifts it and flicks it down in its place. Tico moves: He blows on the domino, then slaps it down with quick force. Jesus moves: no special move. Each player takes another turn. After Jesus' second turn, the men pause.)*

TICO. Did you see that? Who taught him that strategy? Tell me what kid has a game like that?

JELIN. Strategy only goes so far. You have to teach him how to look intimidating when he makes a move.

TICO. He plays it innocent. He makes you think he doesn't have a plan.

JELIN. *(To Jesus.)* Watch your uncle and learn. You have to create your own kind of move. If you want to be king of this game, you have to have style. *(Jelin slides the domino across the table and then, with decisive force, flicks it down.)*

SCENE 3

An old port city on the island. A bustling square in the middle of town, lined with historic buildings. Jesus wanders on, followed by Jelin.

JELIN. I told you to stay where I could see you. Don't go running off.
JESUS. How come they got so many people here?
JELIN. What kind of a question is that?
JESUS. Look at these signs. We need signs like this in Magdalena. Ours are embarrassing, all scribbled and made out of old cardboard. We need some neon signs. We need some fancy stuff.
JELIN. Check it out. It's a tattoo parlor. In the window, you can watch them drawing tattoos on people. They take a big needle, put some color on the tip, and pah!, stick it under your skin. If you get lucky, maybe they're putting one on a woman's ass.
JESUS. Ew.
JELIN. You'll appreciate that one day.
JESUS. Papi has one on his *nalga*. But don't tell him I said that.
JELIN. I was there when he got it put on. He cried like a baby.
JESUS. Mami said it's a sin to have a tattoo. She said if you have one, you can't be buried like a normal dead person. You can only be buried in shame.
JELIN. That woman is always telling stories. God doesn't have time to be bothered with the small stuff.
JESUS. Sure he does.
JELIN. He has to keep the whole world running. You think he cares about a cheap tattoo on your father's ass?
JESUS. You're probably right.
JELIN. Of course I am.
JESUS. *(Pointing.)* Look at that sign. It's made out of gold.
JELIN. That's El Castillo.
JESUS. El Castillo.
JELIN. It's the oldest building on the island. It used to be a convent where all the nuns lived. But now they made it into a five-star hotel. The rooms have enormous beds. The pillows are bigger than

your whole body. When you eat there, they give you a separate fork for your salad, your meat, and your rice.
JESUS. Do they get real important people staying there?
JELIN. Only the rich. They make sure of that.
JESUS. What about the president?
JELIN. We don't have a president.
JESUS. Why not?
JELIN. Because we have a dictator.
JESUS. I don't mean us. I mean the president of America.
JELIN. Sure. He stays in the presidential suite.
JESUS. You watch. I'm going to stay there one day. I'll bring mami, so she can sleep on the big bed. You can come too. You and me will go to the bar, buy some beers, curse about politics.
JELIN. Is that how grown men behave?
JESUS. We'll comb our moustaches. Drive up in fancy cars.
JELIN. And how do you plan to become one of the rich people?
JESUS. I'll get some money from papi.
JELIN. He doesn't have that kind of money.
JESUS. You don't know.
JELIN. Who's older, you or me?
JESUS. You.
JELIN. Then I know.
JESUS. I saw his money. He hides it in the rice barrels.
JELIN. What's he got? A barrel full of rusty old pennies?
JESUS. Once he opened one and showed me how to count to a hundred. He always says, don't spend it. Don't touch it. Don't look at it. Don't tell no one about it.
JELIN. You're telling me.
JESUS. I can trust you with my secrets.
JELIN. Anyway you can't dip into your father's stupid rice barrel. Real men have to earn their own money.
JESUS. I can be like Tico and open a store.
JELIN. Or be a farmer like me and your father.
JESUS. No. I want a sign with my name. A neon sign or a gold sign. *(A carnival performer emerges. It is Yemaya. She is young, heavy, and breathtakingly beautiful. Her skin is the richest shade of brown. She wears a regal blue dress adorned with cowries, silver lace, and duck feathers. Underneath the full skirt, her large hips sway like waves. She approaches Jesus and Jelin. Jelin is aroused.)*
JELIN. Good afternoon, señorita.
JESUS. Whoa. Look at her.

JELIN. Shh. *(To Yemaya.)* Don't mind him.
JESUS. Is there a carnival?
JELIN. Use your brain. What do you think?
YEMAYA. *(She plucks a duck feather from her dress and ruffles it in Jesus' hair.)* You like carnivals?
JESUS. *(He fixes his hair.)* They're okay.
YEMAYA. Oh. Then maybe I should go perform somewhere else.
JELIN. He loves carnivals.
YEMAYA. *(She places a cup before her, for collecting tips.)* For the spirits. *(Jelin and Jesus put some change in her cup. Yemaya performs.)*

    Remember me like you remember your ancestors
    memory more vast than your human years
    search back to the treasures in your birth
    and find me there
    Many of your ancestors were buried in my belly
    blue eyes lie blind in my water
    brown eyes lie blind in my water
    in my dark water they are all the same,
    the eyes of your ancestors
    Do not forget me
    come back to me
    and I will slay your enemies
    I will crusade for your comfort
    I will swallow those who spite you
    I will leave your enemies crying in shame
    Then when death comes
    you will see through the eyes of your parents
    you will see through the eyes
    that saw before you
    you will speak through an eternal voice
(Touching him with the feather on "my children.")
    My children move in broad strokes
    across this mortal world
    just as my tide travels the large surface of the earth
    But my tide is regular
    and returns to the same shores
    So do the hearts of my children
    return to me
    to the breast of Yemaya.
(Her performance is over. She takes her change cup. Just as she exits, Jesus follows her and snatches the duck feather from her hand.)

JELIN. Jesus, how dare you! Why the hell…? Don't you ever touch a woman like that. Do you understand me? I'm talking to you.
JESUS. Yes, tio.
JELIN. You want to be a rich man? You want to stay at El Castillo? Then you better learn to behave like a gentleman, not a stupid-minded little boy. What do you say?
JESUS. I'm sorry. I won't do that again.
JELIN. Give it to me. *(Jesus hands Jelin the feather. Ritual: Jelin holds the feather. He puts it to his nose and, with a large nasal inhale, he smells it. That's how a woman smells. He puts it back to his nose and sniffs four staccato inhales in a row. Fruit. Fish. Saltwater. Blood. He touches the feather to his nipples, tickling and teasing them. He drags the feather down his torso and finally to his crotch, where he brushes the feather. End ritual. Jesus interrupts Jelin, imitating a very loud sniff.)*
JESUS. What does it smell like?
JELIN. Fruit. Fish.
JESUS. Ew.
JELIN. None of your business. If you're anything like your uncle, you'll get it one day.
JESUS. I think she liked you. She was giving you the eyes.
JELIN. Now I'm late for my meeting.
JESUS. Let me hold it. *(Jelin hands him the feather.)*
JELIN. Don't lose it.
JESUS. It's mine anyway.
JELIN. I'll be done soon. Don't leave the square. And keep your hands to yourself. *(Jelin exits. Jesus smells the feather, searching for what it is that Jelin had found there.)*

SCENE 4

Later. Jesus walks into Lila's Grocery on the square, feather in hand. There is a food counter with some stools. Jesus checks out the place, takes a seat.

LILA. Hello there, little man. What can I do for you?
JESUS. Nothing. Thank you.
LILA. Need a snack?

JESUS. Just looking around.
LILA. This is a grocery store, not a museum.
JESUS. Is this your place?
LILA. You see that sign out there? What's it say?
JESUS. L-I-L ...
LILA. Lila's Grocery. That's me.
JESUS. Impressive sign.
LILA. It was the cheapest one I could find.
JESUS. Then I bet you didn't look in Magdalena. Believe me, where I come from they make them much cheaper.
LILA. You going to buy something?
JESUS. You keep it pretty clean in here.
LILA. Hey, you going to buy something?
JESUS. I'm waiting for my uncle.
LILA. If you're not going to buy something then wait for him outside. *(Pause. He demonstrates the feather.)*
JESUS. I don't have any money. You want this?
LILA. Cash only.
JESUS. *(Bargaining.)* It smells like fruit.
LILA. Let me have a look. But no promises. *(He hands her the feather. She inspects it meticulously, messing around.)* I don't know. It's missing some fluff right here.
JESUS. It's from the dress of a queen.
LILA. The queen of what?
JESUS. Shoot. I didn't ask her.
LILA. Then how do you know she was a queen?
JESUS. If you smell it, it'll put you in a trance.
LILA. *(She smells the feather.)* Wait a second ... Hmmm ... Hmmmmmmm ... Hmmmmmmmmmmmm ... Nope. No trance.
JESUS. I think she was the queen of the ocean.
LILA. The whole ocean, or one rinky-dink beach somewhere?
JESUS. The whole thing.
LILA. This will get you one drink. How's a Coke sound?
JESUS. Yes, please.
LILA. Coming right up.
JESUS. I'm planning on opening a grocery store.
LILA. A man with an agenda.
JESUS. I'm going to make enough money to stay at that hotel. El Castillo.
LILA. You think I have that kind of money?
JESUS. You don't?

17

LILA. None of your business.
JESUS. I want a sign like yours except with my name. In my store if the kids are good, they get a free cookie.
LILA. That's no good. Let me give you some advice. You have to think like a businessman.
JESUS. You mean a business lady?
LILA. Rule number one. Nothing is free. Never give something for nothing.
JESUS. You've been in the business a long time, haven't you?
LILA. I've got an official business proposition for you. But only if you're serious about owning a grocery store. *(Pause.)* Well?
JESUS. I'll listen to your proposal.
LILA. When you're all grown up, come back and find me. You can buy this store from me. You get your sign. I take off to a secret location where no one can bother me.
JESUS. I like this store. I would definitely consider buying it.
LILA. *(She puts a bottle on the counter.)* Here's your Coke.
JESUS. Thank you. *(He picks up the bottle, but startled, he drops it on the ground.)* Ow!
LILA. What happened?
JESUS. It stung me!
LILA. What? *(She starts to clean it up.)* What a damn mess.
JESUS. It stung my hand when I touched it.
LILA. Honey, a bottle of Coke can't sting you. Look, I'm touching it and it isn't stinging me. Now feel it and tell me what's wrong with it.
JESUS. *(He feels the bottle, pulls his hand away.)* Why does it feel like that?
LILA. You mean cold?
JESUS. Oh.
LILA. It's straight out of the refrigerator.
JESUS. I didn't drop it on purpose.
LILA. Have you ever had a Coke before? *(Pause.)* Do you know what a refrigerator is?
JESUS. Of course I do.
LILA. What is it?
JESUS. It's a thing that makes things sting.
LILA. Do they have electricity where you're from?
JESUS. I don't know.
LILA. So you don't drink your milk cold?
JESUS. Ew! Cold milk?

LILA. Let me fill you in on a little secret. Everyone outside your no-name town drinks their milk cold and their Coke cold.
JESUS. Magdalena.
LILA. What?
JESUS. That's the name of my town.
LILA. I bet you don't have running water. *(Moment.)*
JESUS. Does the President of America drink things cold?
LILA. He would never drink a warm Coke.
JESUS. I still like it better the normal way.
LILA. It's the country boys like you that turn into stubborn old mules.
JESUS. My papi says that people who live in the city are backwards and twisted.
LILA. Look at me and tell me where I'm twisted. *(He looks at her. Nothing is twisted.)* Your father doesn't know everything. You learn the important stuff on your own, when your parents aren't around. I bet your father never showed you how to buy a Coke with a feather. Right? *(She sniffs the feather again. She retrieves another Coke bottle.)* Here. But drink it outside. If you drop it, you're on your own.
JESUS. But you said, rule number one, never give something for nothing.
LILA. Nothing? I got a feather and a good laugh.
JESUS. Can I still come back?
LILA. For what?
JESUS. To buy the store.
LILA. A deal's a deal.
JESUS. Let's shake on it. *(They shake.)*
LILA. Little Mulo. The stubborn one. Be very careful. The bottle's cold.

SCENE 5

A minute later. Jesus stands outside of Lila's Grocery. The bottle of Coke is in his hand. Ritual: Jesus holds the bottle of Coke in one hand. When the cold starts to burn that hand, he switches to the other and shakes out the burning hand for relief. He puts the bottle to his lips. He pulls it away. He sticks his tongue into the rim of the bottle. He licks the rim of the bottle. He sticks his tongue against the side of the bottle. He puts the bottle back to his lips and takes a gulp. He swishes the soda around rapidly in his mouth, puffing out his cheeks, and then swallows. His eyes widen. A smile slowly forms across his face. He starts gulping down the Coke. End ritual. Jelin enters in a panic.

JELIN. Where the hell were you?
JESUS. I went into the store.
JELIN. I said don't go anywhere.
JESUS. Look, I got a refrigerator Coke. You want to try a sip?
JELIN. We're going back home.
JESUS. I didn't pay for it. I just gave her the feather.
JELIN. Put it down. The bus leaves in a few minutes.
JESUS. But you were going to show me more signs. You said the movie theater has the best sign.
JELIN. Listen. Magdalena is having a fire. They need water.
MULO. What's better? The movie theater sign or El Convento sign?
JELIN. Oye! Have you ever seen a big fire?
JESUS. What's on fire?
JELIN. Some houses.
JESUS. My house is on fire?
JELIN. Some farms. I don't know. A lot of things.
JESUS. Is the fire everywhere?
JELIN. No more questions.
JESUS. Are mami and papi on fire?
JELIN. Did you hear me?
JESUS. But it took us forever to get here. What if mami and papi get burned before we get home?
JELIN. *(Referring to the Coke bottle.)* What is this?

JESUS. A refrigerator Coke.
JELIN. Put it down and let's go.
JESUS. Do you know what a refrigerator is?
JELIN. God damn it, give it to me! *(He rips the bottle from Jesus' hand.)*
JESUS. There was still some left. *(Jelin throws the Coke bottle to the ground.)*

SCENE 6

Weeks later in Magdalena. After the fire. A dark place. Jesus' mother lies on the ground, still. Jesus sits beside her.

JESUS. I got some oil to rub your skin. Does it still hurt here? *(He gently massages her side.)* Yesterday you made noises when I touched you here. Why don't you make some noises now? *(He pokes at her side, seeing if she'll make a noise.)* It's aloe and some other kind of stuff. Special stuff for the burns. Doña Aye made it for you. You put it on the skin, then you move your fingertips in little circles. Like you used to when I was sick. You would rub that tingly stuff on my chest. You would move your fingertips in little circles. It stunk, and then I would fall asleep and dream like I was flying over the mountains.

Can you hear me?

Are you still dreaming about ghosts?

Do you just dream at night or are you dreaming all the time now?

You should eat. *(He tries feeding her. There's no response.)* I'll sing you a song. How about the one we used to sing on the farm and try to bother papi while he worked. When he was grumpy. *(He sings a lullaby.)*

    I'm going to the sea
    To meet my secret love
    If she remembers me
    The sun
    The sun
    The sun

(At the tune, Mami rises from the floor. She sings along. They have a little dance they do when they sing this song.)
MAMI.
> I'll sing her all my songs
> And as the words are sung
> They'll dance within her waves
> The sun
> The sun
> The sun

JESUS and MAMI.
> The sun lives at the edge of the sea
> The sun said she would wait there for me
> The sun …

MAMI.
> I'm going to the sea
> To argue with the rain
> And when the clouds are gone
> The sun
> The sun
> The sun

(Mami twirls offstage.)
JESUS. Mami? *(He looks at the spot where she had been lying on the ground.)* I think you're dreaming all the time.

SCENE 7

> *Night in Magdalena. Darkness. Jesus and Jelin, digging graves. Jesus picks at the dirt with his shovel. Jelin is strong, an experienced digger.*

JESUS. I hate this place.
JELIN. God damnit. What did I just say?
JESUS. You're not supposed to use that word at a cemetery.
JELIN. That's right. I'm sorry. *(Silence as they dig.)*
JESUS. You're not supposed to use that word anywhere.
JELIN. At a funeral you are quiet. You respect the dead. *(Silence as they dig.)*

JESUS. This isn't a real funeral.
JELIN. You bow your head down and say goodbye. *(Silence as they dig.)*
JESUS. You're supposed to read from the Bible and the dead person is in a nice wooden box. And they already dug the hole ahead of time. And the men carry the box through town so the people can see and say goodbye.
JELIN. That's not how everyone does it. That's for lucky people. *(Silence as they dig. Jesus starts picking at the dirt oddly.)*
JESUS. Look. There's worms and bugs all over the place.
JELIN. Bugs only like the dirt. They don't touch the dead people.
JESUS. Yes they do.
JELIN. They're afraid of them. They won't touch your mother.
JESUS. Mami would say this kind of funeral is a sin.
JELIN. To her everything was a sin. Breathing was a sin. Eating was a sin. Smiling, being alive. *(Silence as they dig.)* Dig! Watch what you're doing and pay attention! Don't play with the dirt. You've hardly gone six inches. We'll be out here all night.
JESUS. It hurts my arm.
JELIN. Look how I do it. You hold the shovel one hand on top, one in the middle. Put it in the dirt. Push it in with your foot. Turn the shovel and throw the dirt behind you. *(Jesus follows the instruction.)* That's right. Be precise and strong. Don't pick at it like chicken feed. You have to learn to use your strength. *(Jesus digs more precisely.)* Good. That's the way it's done. *(Jesus' digging becomes more focused and consistent.)* When my mother died, your father and I dug the grave. Our father, your grandfather, he tried to help but he was crying the whole time. He dug with his back to us so we couldn't see. We could tell. His eyes were red and puffy. When he died, your father and me dug the grave. Just the two of us. We didn't march through town. We didn't have money to pay the priest. Then after the fire, I buried your father alone. But I thought you should be here for your mother. She would like that. *(Jesus digs with increasing focus and precision.)* Sometimes you have to be like my father was. You want to cry but you turn your back and hide it. You don't let the world see. *(Jesus digs.)* When we're done, you can say something nice you remember about her. A story or something. That can be your prayer. *(Jesus digs stronger.)* Tomorrow we'll make a cross for the graves. We'll write their names on it. Okay? *(Jesus digs stronger.)* Answer me! *(Jesus digs stronger.)* Answer me or I'll whack you! *(Jesus hurls the shovel at his uncle. He lunges at Jelin and*

shoves him violently. Jelin stumbles.) Go home.
JESUS. Where is that now?

SCENE 8

A new day. Dark morning in Magdalena. Tico sits at his crate. His shirt looks charred and ashy. Mulo, formerly Jesus, enters. He is dragging a barrel behind him using a piece of rope.

TICO. Good morning, Jesus. We missed you around here.
MULO. Don't call me Jesus. It's not my name anymore.
TICO. Oh yeah? What are they calling you these days?
MULO. Jesus is the name my parents gave me and I decided to change it.
TICO. I see.
MULO. You can call me Mulo now.
TICO. That's a weird name.
MULO. It's what a nice woman called me one time.
TICO. I don't think she was being nice if she called you a mule.
MULO. You weren't there.
TICO. So, Mulo, what's with the barrel?
MULO. I'm going to the city on business.
TICO. The bus doesn't come around until sunset.
MULO. As long as it comes.
TICO. It looks like you packed enough stuff.
MULO. It's money.
TICO. All right! I love money! Any in there for me?
MULO. No.
TICO. Let me get you a drink.
MULO. I'll have a coconut. And I'll open it myself.
TICO. Careful. *(Tico hands Mulo a coconut. Mulo holds it down with one hand. In four perfect, precise strokes, he creates a hole in the top.)* You did it. You've been practicing haven't you?
MULO. I need a straw. *(Tico slips a straw into the hole.)*
TICO. If you can open a coconut, you can drink a little rum with it.
MULO. Really?
TICO. Just a drop.

MULO. I thought you're only supposed to drink at night.
TICO. Who told you that? It's never too early. *(Tico pours some rum into the coconut and hands it to Mulo. Mulo gulps and makes a face like it tastes strong.)* So how long are you going to be away on this big business trip?
MULO. Forever. I'm moving to the city.
TICO. Do you have family there?
MULO. I don't have family any more.
TICO. Hey. Don't you ever say that. I'm your family. This town is your family.
MULO. *(He's drunk.)* This town? Before, the sun would rise and I would bring papi his cup of coffee. Now it's dark in the morning. The sun doesn't bother. The roosters don't know what time of day it is. Everyone's dead.
TICO. What about your Uncle Jelin?
MULO. Your wife is dead. *(Moment.)*
TICO. The city is no place for a boy to be on his own. Hey, you want to hear a story?
MULO. No.
TICO. It'll cheer you up.
MULO. So?
TICO. Baldomera used to drag me to her Pentecostal meetings over at her brother's farm. Those damn Pentecostals.
MULO. I heard this one.
TICO. The one where —
MULO. I'll have some more. *(Tico pours some more rum.)*
TICO. You're my only competition at dominoes. If you leave, then what am I supposed to do?
MULO. You can still play Jelin.
TICO. He's an idiot who thinks he's hot shit. I need a challenge or it's no fun.
MULO. Come visit me in the city and we can play dominoes there.
TICO. Hell no. Those city people don't play dominoes the right way. They have backwards rules. They play that you can match up a double piece with any piece you want. It doesn't matter what number it is.
MULO. No one plays like that.
TICO. I refuse to play dominoes with anyone in the city.
MULO. I'll teach them how to play right when I get there.
TICO. And they don't have good coconuts like I sell them here.
MULO. A coconut is a coconut.

TICO. They have shriveled coconuts with hardly no milk in them. You crack them open and sand pours out. They're always bringing in things from the outside. All they drink is Coke.
MULO. I like Coke.
TICO. Sure you do. You're a boy. But let me tell you. Coke is not on the same level as coconuts and dominoes. It never can be and it never will be. It's the natural hierarchy of the world.
MULO. I'm not a boy.
TICO. Jesus, you're not old enough to take care of yourself.
MULO. It's Mulo.
TICO. We have a responsibility to remember the beauty of Magdalena. What about the river? You used to spy on the girls swimming. And the mornings? I was there the first time you counted to ten.
MULO. Ten morning stars.
TICO. You would run around scaring the tree frogs.
MULO. They peed in my hand.
TICO. What about those mornings on the farm when you brought your father coffee?
MULO. I don't remember that.
TICO. I remember it for you. The city has no memories. Did you think about where you're going to stay? How are you going to eat? Things aren't free.
MULO. I have money.
TICO. Things are more expensive there.
MULO. This barrel has all my papi's savings.
TICO. Open it up and let me see.
MULO. I can't get it open. The fire made it stuck closed.
TICO. Give it to me. *(Tico pries open the barrel, looks inside.)*
MULO. Let me see my money.
TICO. Jesus.
MULO. Mulo.
TICO. Why don't you stay with me for a few days? I'll give you a job here at the stand. You already know how to do my inventory. You can be my assistant.
MULO. You want to steal my money.
TICO. It's not money.
MULO. Give it to me.
TICO. The barrel is full of rice.
MULO. It's hidden under the rice. Did you look under the rice?
TICO. It's all rice.

MULO. Liar. *(Mulo reaches his arm into the barrel. It's all rice.)* Every night you go to sleep, you lay down on your family's ashes. When you breathe, it's your wife. When you walk you can feel her under your feet. You don't know what's a burned blanket and what's your wife's skin. You can't tell if it's the ashes from a book or your wife's hair.
TICO. Don't talk about Baldomera that way.
MULO. You breathe her in. You walk on her. You sleep on her. You go to the bathroom on her.
TICO. Go and wait for the bus somewhere else.
MULO. Look at this place, there's ashes everywhere. Ashes on your footprints. Look at your shirt. People's ashes on your shirt. It could be hers.
TICO. Get out of here.
MULO. Fine. *(Mulo starts to leave.)*
TICO. Wait. Give me some rice to pay for your drink. You're a man. You learn to pay. *(Mulo scoops some rice into the coconut husk and hands it to him.)*
MULO. There.
TICO. The bus stops another mile down the road. *(Mulo drags his barrel off. Tico speaks after him.)* You should consider yourself lucky. At least your mother had a body. She had a burial. You should thank god for that. You don't know the difference between a blessing and a curse. *(Mulo's gone. Tico speaks to himself.)* This rice is my wife's ashes. I'll remember her voice that way. Her cooking. Her beautiful skin. Her dark skin. Her mulata hair in braids. She is not ashes. She is rice. I'll speak to her through the rice. Here's her heart. It can be so soft and so hard. Here's her body, and she doesn't have to be buried. I can carry her by my side. *(Ritual: He holds the coconut husk over his head and turns it upside down. Rice pours down over his head, shoulders, and falls to the ground. Then the husk is empty. He kneels to the ground and touches the rice around him. He lies on the ground, on top of the rice. He spots one grain of rice, puts it in his mouth and swallows it whole. End ritual.)* Baldomera.

SCENE 9

Lila's Grocery. Lila is sweeping rice off the floor. Mulo enters dragging the barrel.

LILA. Hello there, little man. That's quite a load. Is that a barrel on a rope? *(Mulo doesn't know what to say.)* Why don't you have a seat? It looks like your feet could use a rest. *(He doesn't know what to say.)* What can I get for you today?
MULO. I came to buy the store.
LILA. Speak up, honey. I'm not going to hurt you.
MULO. I came to buy the store.
LILA. What was that?
MULO. You don't remember me.
LILA. Don't take it personally. I get so many faces coming through here. In and out. So what's with the barrel?
MULO. It's full of money.
LILA. So I got a rich man in my store.
MULO. That's right.
LILA. What is it, rusty old pennies? Toy money?
MULO. And some rice.
LILA. You want some beans to go with that rice?
MULO. My house had a fire.
LILA. *(Moment.)* You're not from Magdalena? Where they had that big fire? *(Moment.)* You're the boy who got burned by the soda bottle. See, I couldn't forget a face as sweet as yours. What happened to your family?
MULO. My mami had bandages on her face.
LILA. Come here and I'll give you a hug for her. *(Lila takes Mulo into her arms.)*
MULO. Do they play dominoes here in the city?
LILA. They play right outside in the square.
MULO. But do they play with weird rules?
LILA. We play by the normal rules.
MULO. I like the rules my uncle taught me.
LILA. Was your uncle hurt in the fire?
MULO. Do you sell coconuts here?

LILA. We got some right over there.
MULO. You have to cut a hole in the top for a drink. That's how they do it in the country.
LILA. Listen, what's-your-name, this isn't a shelter. *(Mulo clears his throat.)*
MULO. I'm following up on our deal. All I have is this rice but I would like to buy your store.

SCENE 10

Sunrise at Lila's Grocery. Mulo is asleep on the floor. A girl shouts from outside.

MAYA. Good morning! *(Maya taps on the door.)* Hello? *(She bangs on the door.)* Hey, on the floor. Are you open? *(She imitates the morning call of a rooster. Mulo pops awake and lets her in.)*
MULO. How did you do that?
MAYA. Knocking didn't work.
MULO. I thought you were a rooster.
MAYA. Why are you sleeping on the floor like a stray dog?
MULO. It's my new bed.
MAYA. It's not a bed. It's the floor.
MULO. I used to sleep in a hammock, but they're not so great. You can tip over and fall out of them. On the floor you can't fall down.
MAYA. You can't fall down if you're already at the bottom. *(Moment.)*
MULO. Hello and welcome to Lila's Grocery. How can I help you?
MAYA. I need two cases of Spam.
MULO. Let's see. *(He peruses a sheet of paper.)* According to my inventory, we have less than one case in stock. Do you want to place an order?
MAYA. As long as I can get it by the end of the week.
MULO. I have to check with my boss. What is that Spam anyway?
MAYA. It's meat in a can.
MULO. What kind of meat?
MAYA. American meat.
MULO. Is it as good as a refrigerator Coke?
MAYA. What?

MULO. A refrigerator Coke. It's a cold drink. It stings you and tastes good at the same time. It's like pleasure and pain all mixed up in your mouth. *(He retrieves a Coke bottle.)* You want one?
MAYA. You mean, a refrigerated Coke.
MULO. You want to feel it?
MAYA. No, just the Spam.
MULO. Don't you get sick of meat-in-a-can?
MAYA. My mother used to have it on her boat.
MULO. She was a fisherman?
MAYA. I don't like boys who ask a lot of questions.
MULO. It's important to be friends with my customers.
MAYA. It's top secret. She took people on boat rides to America. She took Spam because the meat never spoils.
MULO. Did you go with her?
MAYA. Sometimes.
MULO. So you actually went inside of America?
MAYA. They have a hundred kinds of Coke there.
MULO. What? I thought there's only one kind.
MAYA. They have a thousand kinds of meat in a can.
MULO. Have you tasted them all?
MAYA. You could live there all your life and you still wouldn't have enough time to taste everything.
MULO. I'd eat a different kind of meat-in-a-can every day until I had tasted every single kind. And I'd drink a different kind of Coke each time to wash it down. Do they have Coke flavored like a coconut?
MAYA. I don't think so.
MULO. If there's a hundred flavors one of them has to be coconut. It's one of the basics.
MAYA. The flavors are different than the kind we have here. They have dark cherry. Lemon. Orange. Blueberry. Chocolate. Vanilla. Flavors like that.
MULO. Coconut Coke. Coconut Coca-Cola. Coco-cola. Cocola. Cola-coco. Cona-loco. Coca-nola. Co. Ca. No. La. Coca-nola! I'm going to invent it. The president of America is going to love it better than any other flavor.
MAYA. Maybe you'll make a fortune and you won't have to sleep on the floor anymore.
MULO. I'll sleep in fancy hotels. *(Maya sees the duck feather displayed on the counter.)*
MAYA. What's this for?

MULO. It's from the queen of the ocean.
MAYA. I'm not impressed. *(Maya picks up the feather. She inspects it. She smells it. In a teasing, sensual manner, she puts it down her shirt and under her bra.)*
MULO. That's stealing.
MAYA. Are you going to tell on me? *(Lila enters.)*
LILA. You opened the store without me?
MULO. We had a customer.
LILA. I'm sorry. What can I do for you?
MAYA. The little boy was helping me.
MULO. She put in an order for two cases of Spam.
MAYA. I need it by the end of the week.
LILA. That shouldn't be a problem.
MAYA. What's the price?
LILA. Ten cents a can.
MAYA. They used to be less.
LILA. They're twice as much down the street.
MAYA. Only one case, then. I'll be in on Friday to pick it up. *(Maya exits.)*
MULO. I had my first customer. Here's the order slip. One case of Spam by Friday. High priority.
LILA. You don't open the store unless I'm here.
MULO. I could barely sleep last night. The neon is really bright. The men were playing dominoes in the square. When are you going to teach me the city rules?
LILA. We have more important things to take care of.
MULO. I stayed up and made lists of everything you sell. It's called inventory. *(He pulls out a piece of paper and reads from it.)* Bottles of Coke, twenty eight. Eleven in the refrigerator, seventeen on the shelf. Egg cartons, eight. Cans of pigeon peas, nineteen. You're low on bread. Only four rolls.
LILA. Slow down a minute.
MULO. Cans … of … green … peas …
LILA. Let me see. *(He hands her the inventory.)* Half these things aren't spelled right.
MULO. I wrote it late. I was tired.
LILA. It doesn't matter how many pigeon peas we have.
MULO. My friend Tico runs a business and he said you have to keep track of things.
LILA. Is he from Magdalena?
MULO. Why?

LILA. Was he hurt in the fire?
MULO. I don't know.
LILA. This weekend the two of us will take a drive to Magdalena and pay him a visit.
MULO. We should stay here so I can see what the weekend business is like.
LILA. We'll go on Sunday when the store is closed.
MULO. Now that you have me here, we can stay open on Sunday.
LILA. Does your uncle know where you are?
MULO. I don't have any uncles.
LILA. You said you did.
MULO. We should sit down today and discuss our deal. How much I have to pay you for the store. When we can add my name to the sign. How we'll split the work. Unless you want to retire altogether.
LILA. Mulo, I could barely pay you in pennies.
MULO. How many pennies?
LILA. You can't just sleep on the floor. Magdalena's only a few hours away.
MULO. I have to wash the windows.
LILA. Not on Sunday you don't.
MULO. I have to get things ready for Monday.
LILA. Your uncle's probably looking all over for you.
MULO. I have to stay here and clean the refrigerator. I have to polish the sign. What will people think if the windows aren't clean on Monday?
LILA. I'm not bargaining with you.
MULO. Fine. If you want to cheat and break your deal. You want to send me back to the ashes. There's still burned dogs in the street. And bugs in the dirt. You can leave me with the bugs.
LILA. We're finding your family.
MULO. Worms in the dirt. *(Moment. Lila gets the dominoes.)*
LILA. How about I teach you those city rules now? *(Moment.)*
MULO. I was very good at the country rules. If it's anything similar, I'll probably beat you.
LILA. First thing, you make a bet. In the city, we only play when there's money on the table.
MULO. All I have is rice.
LILA. *(She hands him some pennies.)* Here's some pay for taking care of the inventory.
MULO. Can you bet things other than money?
LILA. You can bet whatever.

MULO. If I win, we don't ever go to Magdalena. I open the store on Sunday and you get a day off.
LILA. And if I win, we go find your uncle.
MULO. I also bet three pennies. Soon my barrel will be full of money. *(Lila deals out the dominoes. Jesus goes first. He now has a "move." He puts the domino on the table face down and quickly flips it over, revealing his play. Lila moves. She holds the domino in the opponent's face and then slams it on the table. They continue to play in silence.*

Sunrise in Magdalena

Tico is asleep on the floor under his bar. The coconut husk that holds his wife's rice is curled in his arms. Jelin walks in and slowly, without disturbing Tico, peeks into the coconut husk.

JELIN. Service! Service! *(Tico wakes up.)* Can a man get some service around here?
TICO. Closed for business. How many times do I have to tell you?
JELIN. You can't be closed on a day like today. We have to celebrate.
TICO. I was asleep. It was peaceful.
JELIN. The government farm scientist guy came through.
TICO. Let me guess. They're not giving us any aid.
JELIN. Next year at this time, our farms will be doing better than ever. The fire burned away all the crappy old dirt. The dirt underneath is more fertile. It's nutrient-rich.
TICO. Next year? I'm hungry now. I can't wait a year to eat a yam.
JELIN. Pull out the dark rum and let's have a toast.
TICO. You finished off my dark rum yesterday.
JELIN. We only need a drop.
TICO. The bottle's dry.
JELIN. How about some light rum, then?
TICO. It exploded in the fire.
JELIN. Did all your beers explode, too?
TICO. You want a bottle or a can?
JELIN. Bottle.
TICO. No more bottles.
JELIN. Well then a can.
TICO. All out of cans.
JELIN. Bullshit. I know you got something back there. You owe me ten bucks from dominoes. Give me the beer and I'll reduce your debt to five.

TICO. What beer?
JELIN. You can't lie to save your life.
TICO. I've got the best poker face around.
JELIN. Oh yeah? Let's see. *(Jelin looks Tico in the eye.)* Based on your brilliant poker face, I say you've got one … bottle … of lager behind the bar.
TICO. Don't do this to me.
JELIN. That's some poker face!
TICO. Who do they think they are to come and tell us the fire was a good thing? They walk into a widow's home and say, you're a very lucky woman. It's an excuse not to give us any aid.
JELIN. We'll play dominoes. If I win, I get the beer. If I win twice in a row, I get the beer and the rice.
TICO. What rice?
JELIN. The rice you got hidden in that coconut. You were hugging it like a baby. We'll have a beer and rice feast!
TICO. It's not rice for eating.
JELIN. What's it for then?
TICO. For having around.
JELIN. I'm a master at cooking rice.
TICO. If it was for eating, I would have had it a week ago when I ran out of food. *(Tico pulls out the dominoes. He deals and they begin to play. Their play overlaps with Mulo and Lila's game.)* Any word from Jesus? *(Jelin moves. Tico stops playing.)*
JELIN. It's your move. *(Tico holds his domino, waiting for an answer.)*
TICO. Go find him.
JELIN. Are we playing dominoes or discussing my personal matters? *(The men play in silence. Lila makes her winning move.)*
MULO. That's not fair.
LILA. See, it's not so different than the country rules.
MULO. If it was country rules I would have won.
LILA. We go find your family.
MULO. One more game.
LILA. You learned your first real lesson in the city. Never bet high unless you know what you're doing. *(She takes his pennies from the table.)*

SCENE 11

Lila's Grocery. The end of the week. Mulo and Maya are in the store.

MULO. One case of meat-in-a-can.
MAYA. How much does it cost?
MULO. How much does it cost to go to America?
MAYA. I said, what do I owe you?
MULO. Please. I need to go on the boat with you. I have to leave soon.
MAYA. Will you be quiet? Don't just blurt it out so everyone can hear. You can't use the words "boat" or "America."
MULO. I'm good at keeping secrets.
MAYA. It costs a lot of money. You have to plan it in advance.
MULO. The woman who owns this place says I'm a stray dog. She's going to make me sleep on the floor forever.
MAYA. The ocean isn't so good for sleeping.
MULO. America is.
MAYA. Don't say that word.
MULO. In that place, there's a hammock waiting for me.
MAYA. They sleep in beds there.
MULO. There's a fancy hotel where I'm going to stay. I'll give you the Spam for free.
MAYA. You mean you'll steal it? What if you're trying to rat me out or something? Maybe you're going to run and tell the police.
MULO. I swear on my mother's spirit. I didn't tell on you for stealing the feather.
MAYA. What happened to your mother? *(Moment.)*
MULO. Two cases, for free.
MAYA. We need drinks.
MULO. Free.
MAYA. Tonight at midnight. There's a blue house at the end of the pier. Light a stick of incense. When you see my signal, return it. That's how fishermen talk to each other at night.
MULO. What about fisherwomen?
MAYA. All the original fishers were women.

MULO. Maybe that's why men like the ocean so much.
MAYA. Men don't like the ocean. They're scared of it, and they like being scared. You don't know about what men like.
MULO. Sure I do. I am one.
MAYA. Then you can bring all the Spam with you tonight so I don't have to carry it. Remember, how fishers talk to each other.
MULO. So no one else can hear.

SCENE 12

Midnight. Sounds of water lapping. Darkness. A light flickers on and off. Another flicker. A signal.

MAYA. Who's there?
MULO. It's Mulo.
MAYA. You got the food? *(Maya flicks on a light just long enough to reveal the Spam, Coke, and Mulo's barrel.)* What's in the barrel?
MULO. That's my personal stuff.
MAYA. The boat's too small. No personal stuff allowed.
MULO. It's my papi's savings.
MAYA. Stuff like that is dangerous on the ocean. The pirates come looking to steal whatever you have.
MULO. Pirates? Are you kidding me? *(Maya flicks on the light and looks inside the barrel.)*
MAYA. Pennies and rice? Even the pirates wouldn't want this. Roll it in the water so it floats away and doesn't blow our cover.
MULO. It's good rice.
MAYA. I'm in charge. Understand? Now, are you coming or should I leave you here with your rice? *(We hear a splashing sound as the barrel is dropped into the water.)* Follow close behind and stay quiet. If you have to cough or sneeze, bunch up your shirt and cough quietly into the fabric. Once you get on the boat, I'll give you a fishing rod. You have to sit upright and carry it like a fisher. When you get tired, we trade and you rest a little.
MULO. I can't see.
MAYA. Hold on to me.
MULO. Do you think my barrel will sink or float? Where will it

float to? *(Water splashes nearby.)* Someone's coming.
MAYA. Calm down. It's the water. Are you ready? *(A voice cuts through the night. An echo that is too close.)*
MAMI. Jesus! *(Mulo stops.)*
MAYA. What are you doing? Come on.
MULO. Did you hear that?
MAYA. It's the frogs. They sound like that at night.
MAMI. Jesus! Come and bring your father his coffee. He said you never brought him the second cup.
MULO. Mami?
MAYA. You're too young to come.
MAMI. Jesus! Did you bring him the coffee? Or were you lazy instead?
MULO. Maya? Where are you?
MAYA. Shh. We're almost there. Now touch the dirt and say goodbye.

SCENE 13

Sunrise on the ocean. Blue water splashes against the boat. Maya opens a can of Spam.

MULO. Does it sting when you eat it?
MAYA. No. For the tenth time.
MULO. Does it have little air bubbles?
MAYA. Here you go. Smell it first. *(He smells the meat.)*
MULO. Does all American meat smell like that?
MAYA. You get used to it. It says here, "Ingredients: Pork with added ham." Scoop some with your fingers. *(She hands him the can. He scoops some out with his fingers and tastes it.)*
MULO. It doesn't taste like refrigerator Coke.
MAYA. Not refrigerator Coke. Just one word. Coke.
MULO. It's not as good as mami's pork chops.
MAYA. But it never goes bad. *(They eat together.)*
MULO. How long til we get to America?
MAYA. It depends. A couple weeks usually.
MULO. What color do they paint the houses? Blue?

MAYA. It's not colors. It's brick.
MULO. What about hotels? What's the name of the fancy hotel?
MAYA. It's like Coke and meat-in-a-can. There's too many for me to name them all.
MULO. Did you ever meet the President of America?
MAYA. No more talking about America. Talk about the water. On a boat you tell water stories.
MULO. I don't know any water stories.
MAYA. Here's one. My mother is a water spirit. *(Pause. Long pause.)*
MULO. And?
MAYA. Her spirit lives at the bottom of the ocean. When there's a storm, I can hear her voice saying my name. *(Longer pause.)*
MULO. That's it?
MAYA. It's impressive.
MULO. That's not how you tell a story. You have to start at the beginning and say a lot of stuff that happens. And you have to give good details. Start over. From the way beginning.
MAYA. There was a woman who lived by the water. A fisherwoman.
MULO. Wait. What kind of fish did she catch?
MAYA. I don't know.
MULO. Make it up.
MAYA. Jellyfish.
MULO. Ew.
MAYA. And she cleaned off the slimy part and cooked arroz con jellyfish.
MULO. Ew. That's good.
MAYA. Her boat was called The Decision. On her boat, she took people to far away countries and continents. Out on the ocean, she caught fish with her bare hands. She scaled and prepared the fish with her strong teeth. Then she lay the fish on her warm belly to cook it. She fed many journeyers this way. On one trip, a man loved the flavor of the fish so much, he fell in love with her. He touched her belly and they kissed. Like this. *(Pause.)* They made a baby on the ocean. The baby grew inside the woman's watery belly, and then was born. She grew to be a gorgeous young woman. Sometimes she went on the boat with her mother. Sometimes she stayed back home by herself and waited for The Decision to appear on the horizon. One time, the girl waited more days than usual. Then more weeks than usual. Every night she stood with her ankles in the sand, waiting. It started to rain. Rain fell in the sand, in the waves. In the rain, she heard her mother's voice calling her name.

"Maya! Maya!"
MULO. What happened to the mami?
MAYA. She sprouted seaweed for hair.
MULO. And the papi?
MAYA. She never met him. She drifts off in a boat to try and find him.
MULO. I think she'll find him.
MAYA. Don't say mami and papi. Say mother and father.
MULO. Mother and father.
MAYA. Now you tell a water story.
MULO.
> Red white and blue
> Sugar and gin
> My story begins

MAYA. What?
MULO. That's how I start. Say it with me.
MAYA and MULO.
> Red white and blue
> Sugar and gin
> My story begins

MULO. When I was a kid, we lived at the top of the highest mountain in the whole world. It was so high up, you could feel a breeze when St. Peter opened heaven's gates to let someone in. Before the sun rose, my father left to water the farm. It was still dark out. The stars were like a thousand blinking eyes. See? *(He blinks his eyes like stars.)* I walked across the farm to bring him coffee. I waited for him to finish, to bring the empty cup back to my mother. While I waited, I looked at his feet. They were dirty and sweaty. All around his ankles, the tiny leaves were covered with little drops of dew. Mixed with the dirt. I used to believe his sweat was part of the dew. I thought, that's how the plants grow, from my father's sweat.

Now here's the end part. Say it with me.
MAYA and MULO.
> Red white and blue
> Sugar and rum
> My story is done

MAYA. Why were you looking at his feet?
MULO. He didn't really talk. I just stood there waiting. Never mind, you don't get it. *(Suddenly Mulo goes to the side of the boat, feeling sick.)* The Spam gave me a stomach ache.

MAYA. You're seasick. The waves are bad right now. It goes away after a couple days. *(Light rain.)*
MULO. Listen. It sounds like tree frogs.
MAYA. It sounds like a storm.
MULO. Can you hear your mother? *(Maya listens.)* Do you ever wish you could sink all the way to the bottom of the ocean and see her again? *(Harsh rain erupts. It sounds like tree frogs. The ocean becomes violent.)*
MAYA. We have to scoop the water out of the boat! *(The storm intensifies. Mulo rises and walks to the edge of the boat. He leans over, feeling the storm push and pull at his gravity.)* Stop fooling around and come help me!
MULO. Don't you want the water to cover you?
MAYA. Grab the food!
MULO. *(Yelling over the storm.)* Hello! Hello! Hello!
    Red white and blue
    Sugar and gin!
    Red white and blue
    Sugar and rum!
MAYA. Don't stand there! A wave could hit! *(Layers of blue thrash in every direction. A blue wave rises and covers Mulo's body. He disappears.)*

SCENE 14

Underwater. Mulo plummets through layers and layers of blue. Down, down, down. Tumbling through bubbles and blue. In the blurry distance, at the ocean floor, Mami sits at a table and plays dominoes alone. She sings to herself. Every so often, she moves, kissing the domino and then placing it down.

MAMI.
    I'm going to the sea
    To meet my secret love
    If she remembers me
    The sun
    The sun
    The sun

I'll sing her all my songs
And as the words are sung
They'll dance within her waves
The sun
The sun
The sun

(Mulo continues to plummet as Mami hums the tune softly. Slowly, a sign comes into view. It is El Castillo, the hotel underwater. Tico is the concierge. He approaches Mulo.)

TICO. Excuse me, sir, are you lost?
MULO. Which way is it to America?
TICO. Right this way, sir.
MULO. Is it to the left or right?
TICO. If you follow me I'll be happy to assist you. *(He leads Mulo into the hotel. Mami is in the lobby, playing dominoes with herself. Mulo sees her.)*
MULO. Who is she?
TICO. Welcome to El Castillo hotel. How can I be of service on this fine day?
MULO. I guess … I would like a room for one, please.
TICO. Wait. I'm sorry. Are you Sr. Mulo? Of course. I'm Tico, the main man. We already have your reservation. The presidential suite. At the risk of being bold, I must tell you. The president of America was furious when he found out you reserved his suite. But what could I do? Sr. Mulo, of course, is the preferred guest. And how long will you be staying with us?
MULO. A hundred days.
TICO. I'll mark you down forever, just in case. Otherwise the president may try to book your room for a later date. Your payment was wired to us, in rice and pennies. Your luggage has arrived and it's quite handsome. *(He points to the entrance, where Mulo's barrel is propped.)* I'll have a porter bring that down to you.
MULO. That would be excellent.
TICO. I have a message for you. An Uncle Jelin is waiting at the bar.
MULO. Send word I'll see him soon.
TICO. Of course.
MULO. *(Mulo points to Mami.)* Who is she?
TICO. Just a lady who plays dominoes.
MULO. Where is she from? *(Jelin enters.)*
JELIN. Hey! Sr. Mulo! I've been waiting forever. This place is horrible without you. There's nothing to do. I got all our preparations

together. They got our drinks ready at the bar. They got our moustache combs. They got forks, knives, and spoons.
MULO. Do they have the big pillows?
JELIN. Wait until you see them. They're enormous. But I have to warn you. The president of America had a tantrum after the presidential suite fiasco.
MULO. Tell him to join us at the bar for some drinks.
JELIN. He's refusing to talk to you.
MULO. Did he try Coca-Nola yet?
JELIN. Rumor has it he can't stop drinking the stuff. His advisors say he has one with every meal, plus a fourth as a late-night cocktail.
MULO. Send him a bottle from my personal collection, along with an invitation to join us at the bar. He can't refuse that.
JELIN. Perfect. He's a sucker for expensive gifts. *(Jelin exits.)*
TICO. Here's your key. Make sure you don't lose it. They're nearly impossible to duplicate down here. *(He hands Mulo the coconut husk.)* To get to your room, take the grand staircase. Follow it down, down, down. As far down as it goes. Your door is the last one on the bottom. That's the penthouse. The presidential suite. It has the most stunning view.
MULO. Down, down, down. As far as it goes.
TICO. As a matter of fact, I'll lead you there. *(They begin to exit. Mami looks up from her dominoes.)*
MAMI. Mulo. Want to play a hand?
MULO. You know my name.
MAMI. Mulo the dominoes legend. They say your strategy can beat anyone.
MULO. Do I know you?
MAMI. The only boy I know is named Jesus. Should I deal you in?
MULO. I don't have any money to put down. My papi was stingy.
MAMI. We don't play for money down here. Ocean rules. It's the jungle or the desert. Life or death. Wind or water. Kiss or stop breathing. Which one are you betting on?
MULO. How do you decide?
MAMI.
    Blue green and gold
    Yucca and corn
    Your memory is born
TICO. Sir? Your room's waiting.
MULO. *(To Mami.)* I have to get settled but I'll be back later. After I meet the President of America. Wait for me. *(Tico disappears*

down the staircase. Mulo follows him but Maya runs into the hotel and grabs his waist.)
MAYA. Remember me like you remember your ancestors.
MULO. Excuse me! I have to comb my moustache.
MAYA. Search back to the treasures in your birth.
MULO. What will the president of America think?
MAYA. Do not forget me.
MAMI. Kiss or stop breathing.
MULO. I have to go all the way to the bottom.
MAYA. Come back to me. *(She kisses him on the lips. He kisses back.)*

SCENE 15

A minute later on the boat. The ocean is still. Mulo lies in Maya's arms. His shirt is gone. His body is limp.

MAYA. Hello? Mulo? Cough once if you can hear me. *(Pause.)* If you don't cough then you're dead and the sharks will come eat you. *(She holds his nose shut. He coughs.)* How many fingers am I holding up?
MULO. Watch out. There's a fish in your fingernail.
MAYA. Saltwater twists the way you see things. You had saltwater coming out of everywhere. Out of your ears and nose. You were spitting it up.
MULO. Blue green and gold. Yucca and corn. Your memory is born. Guess what? I went to heaven.
MAYA. No, our Spam did. And our water did. Our compass. Everything went overboard.
MULO. Can I have some American meat?
MAYA. I told you. It's gone.
MULO. How about meat-in-a-can?
MAYA. We're going to starve.
MULO. Heaven's at the lowest part of the ocean. Where no one's ever been. That's where they keep all the cans and the pork chops. I was about to go to the bottom but then you came and kissed me.
MAYA. It wasn't kissing. It's what you do when people stop breathing.

MULO. I saw the domino woman in the hotel.
MAYA. There's no hotel.
MULO. She said you're pretty and you should kiss me.
MAYA. You don't know anything about kissing.
MULO. That's how they kiss in heaven. In America. Big wet kiss. *(He coughs.)*

SCENE 16

Many days later. Mulo lies limp on the floor of the boat. He is weak, his body is shivering. He is moaning happily, deep in the midst of a sexual dream.

MULO. Ahh.
MAYA. Mulo.
MULO. Ah. Ahh. Ahhh.
MAYA. Oh god.
MULO. Mmmm.
MAYA. Mulo! Wake up!
MULO. Look at her! *(He wakes up.)*
MAYA. You're talking in your sleep again.
MULO. Oh. What an amazing dream.
MAYA. By the sound of it, they've all been pretty amazing lately.
MULO. Poof. Into the air. I wish I could get it back. All men should sleep on the ocean.
MAYA. You're dehydrated and you're having wet dreams.
MULO. Did I miss anything exciting?
MAYA. Some clouds looked like a pineapple. A bird took a shit.
MULO. No American boat came to our rescue?
MAYA. A huge pack of jellyfish floated by. That's what our Spam looked like when sunk in the storm. All those cans like silver jellyfish falling through the waves.
MULO. I feel like a refrigerator. As soon as I wake up I feel my stomach again. *(He moves to the side of the boat, queasy, but nothing comes out.)* There's nothing inside me.
MAYA. The sun won't go away.
MULO. You want to rip this part of you out. *(She feels his forehead*

for a fever.)
MAYA. You have to think of something else. Why don't you tell me what your dream was like?
MULO. A man doesn't tell his secrets.
MAYA. You're not a man yet.
MULO. That's what you think.
MAYA. Then tell me about your manly dream.
MULO. Only if you tell me a secret in return.
MAYA. That's childish.
MULO. Then no deal.
MAYA. Okay, okay.
MULO. In my dream I was walking through the city. Kind of the city, except it was underwater. A woman came up to me. She had these amazing, enormous hips.
MAYA. What was she wearing?
MULO. A blue dress.
MAYA. Oh. I though she might not be wearing anything.
MULO. Her hands looked normal at first. But then I realized, instead of fingertips she had little seashells. She started to touch me with her seashell fingertips.
MAYA. Where?
MULO. I don't remember.
MAYA. I bet you do.
MULO. It felt smooth. Like the skin of an orange. Like the edge of a penny. You know when you cut open a coconut, if you run your finger inside the white part? That's how it felt. Do you think in America the women are beautiful like the woman from my dream?
MAYA. No. They're only that beautiful when you're lost at sea.
MULO. Then I'm glad I'm lost.
MAYA. Am I as beautiful as she was?
MULO. Maybe.
MAYA. Have you ever had a woman touch you?
MULO. Now it's your turn.
MAYA. The way the woman in your dream touched you?
MULO. You have to tell me a secret now.
MAYA. I've touched like that before. With boys on the boat. Show me how she touched you.
MULO. My fingers are all rough. See? *(She touches his fingers.)*
MAYA. I'll pretend.
MULO. I can't do it as good as the woman in my dream.
MAYA. Try. *(He leans his hand out to touch her. She grabs his hand*

45

and holds it still.)
MAYA. Wait. Am I as beautiful as the woman in your dream?
MULO. Maybe. *(Ritual: Mulo reaches his hands out and touches her. His fingers slide up and down her body, making the motion of waves. As he does this, he makes whooshing sounds through his teeth. Mulo puts his fingers to her breasts and pops his fingertips like sea foam. Mulo reaches under her shirt and slowly pulls out the feather from between her breasts. He puts the feather to his nose and smells it. That is how a woman smells. End ritual.)*
MAYA. What does it smell like?
MULO.
>Fruit.
>*(Inhale.)*
>Fish.
>*(Inhale.)*
>Saltwater.
>*(Inhale.)*
>Blood.

SCENE 17

In the boat. Bright sun. Tired skin. Dry lips. Maya and Mulo sit lethargically, little energy left. Mami sits on the surface of the water.

MULO. Hmm?
MAYA. What?
MULO. Don't fall asleep.
MAYA. I'm tired.
MULO. What if you don't wake up?
MAYA. Leave me alone.
MULO. What happens if you don't have a funeral?
MAYA. I don't know.
MULO. I think your soul wanders around and you can never rest.
MAYA. That's what's going to happen to us. We're not getting a funeral. We're going to float forever. Lost.
MULO. No. In America everyone has a real funeral.

MAYA. Wander around forever. Lost and lost and lost.
MULO. Did your mother have a funeral?
MAYA. We never found her body.
MULO. That's why you hear her voice when it rains, Maya. We have to give our mothers a funeral.
MAYA. You can't have a funeral without the body.
MULO. Pretend like the feather is their body. *(He holds up the feather.)* See? It's soft like her hair.
MAYA. Like her belly was.
MULO. Welcome to the funeral of our mothers. We don't have their bodies but this feather stands for them instead.
MAYA. Say their names. Gloria Perez.
MULO. Teresa Morales. *(Mami rises and stands before the feather.)* Now we will say our prayers. St. Peter, I hope you let my mother into heaven. Give her a green tree to sit under when she does the sewing. And give her some pork chops to fry, you won't regret it. And she likes her coffee with no sugar. Amen.
MAYA. Yemaya, queen of the ocean, let my mother speak through a seashell. Like the ones you hear on the beach. That way she can whisper like she used to after I went to bed. But she used to yell a lot, too, so give her some storms and hurricanes every once in a while. Amen. Now what? *(They hold the feather in the air. The wind blows in circles and spirals around them. Water splashes against the boat.)*

Magdalena

Tico is at his bar stand, holding the coconut husk.

TICO. Baldomera. They said to plant whatever we have and it will be the best harvest ever. I'm no farmer, but what else can I do now? The stand is down the drain. After the fire, no one's buying any more. Just making ends meet. But maybe the farming will be good. I can come and farm and talk to you and water the earth. *(He tosses rice onto the ground like seed.)*

The Cemetery

Jelin stands before Mami's grave with a Coke bottle.

JELIN. It's been three weeks now. I found a woman in the city who

saw him. She even took him in for a few nights. But she said he disappeared. An eleven-year-old boy alone in the city. I searched all over. Look. I wrote your name on it. "To Teresa, love your son Jesus." Tico said he liked Coca Cola. I promised Jesus I would put a cross on your grave, but this is even better. *(He places the Coke bottle at the head of the grave. The ocean. The air blows in circles, whistling and spinning. Water and wind all around. Mulo and Maya hold the feather in the air. They let go. Mami catches the feather as it twirls through the air. She walks on the surface of the water, waving the feather as she goes. Mulo and Maya watch as the feather glides into the distance.)*
MAYA. I think it worked.
MULO. They heard us.
MAYA. Mulo, look. Really far away.
MULO. It's the feather.
MAYA. No. It's green. Squint your eyes.
MULO. I don't know. A horse fly sitting on the water.
MAYA. Close one eye and squint the other.
MULO. A mosquito?
MAYA. It's land.
MULO. Is that what land looks like?
MAYA. A little bit of green. White dots where the waves are crashing.
MULO. Is that what America looks like?
MAYA. We're still too far away.
MULO. Try to remember. You've seen it before.
MAYA. I kind of remember it from this far. But it looks like everywhere else too.
MULO. They heard us. Our mothers got us to America.
MAYA. We can't be sure.
MULO. My hair is messed up. What if the president sees me this way?
MAYA. He won't be there. We can't be sure where it is anyway.
MULO.
    Red white and blue
    Sugar and gin
Say it with me.
MAYA and MULO.
    Red white and blue
    Sugar and gin
    Red white and blue
    Sugar and gin

MAYA. Wait. Where'd it go? Do you see it?
MULO.
  Red white and blue
  Sugar and gin
MAYA. It's gone. Look. It disappeared.
MULO.
  It doesn't matter. Just say it with me.
  Red white and blue
  Sugar and gin
MAYA. Open your eyes and look. Help me find it again.
MULO. Come on!
  Red white and blue
  Sugar and gin
  Red white and blue
  Sugar and gin
MULO and MAYA.
  Red white and blue
  Sugar and gin
  Red white and blue
  Sugar and gin
(They repeat this. They move through the wind and the water.)

End of Play

PROPERTIES LIST

Cup of coffee
2 bottles of rum
6 coconuts
Machete
4 bottles of beer
3 straws
A couple of bucks (currency)
Dominoes
Duck feather
Cup
Coke bottles
Oil
Food
Shovels
Barrel on a rope, filled with rice
Inventory list
Pennies
Cans of Spam
Coconut husk filled with rice

SOUND EFFECTS

Water lapping
Rain, storm
Splashing sound
Wind and water

NEW PLAYS

★ **THE GREAT AMERICAN TRAILER PARK MUSICAL music and lyrics by David Nehls, book by Betsy Kelso.** Pippi, a stripper on the run, has just moved into Armadillo Acres, wreaking havoc among the tenants of Florida's most exclusive trailer park. "Adultery, strippers, murderous ex-boyfriends, Costco and the Ice Capades. Undeniable fun." –*NY Post.* "Joyful and unashamedly vulgar." –*The New Yorker.* "Sparkles with treasure." –*New York Sun.* [2M, 5W] ISBN: 978-0-8222-2137-1

★ **MATCH by Stephen Belber.** When a young Seattle couple meet a prominent New York choreographer, they are led on a fraught journey that will change their lives forever. "Uproariously funny, deeply moving, enthralling theatre." –*NY Daily News.* "Prolific laughs and ear-to-ear smiles." –*NY Magazine.* [2M, 1W] ISBN: 978-0-8222-2020-6

★ **MR. MARMALADE by Noah Haidle.** Four-year-old Lucy's imaginary friend, Mr. Marmalade, doesn't have much time for her—not to mention he has a cocaine addiction and a penchant for pornography. "Alternately hilarious and heartbreaking." –*The New Yorker.* "A mature and accomplished play." –*LA Times.* "Scathingly observant comedy." –*Miami Herald.* [4M, 2W] ISBN: 978-0-8222-2142-5

★ **MOONLIGHT AND MAGNOLIAS by Ron Hutchinson.** Three men cloister themselves as they work tirelessly to reshape a screenplay that's just not working—*Gone with the Wind.* "Consumers of vintage Hollywood insider stories will eat up Hutchinson's diverting conjecture." –*Variety.* "A lot of fun." –*NY Post.* "A Hollywood dream-factory farce." –*Chicago Sun-Times.* [3M, 1W] ISBN: 978-0-8222-2084-8

★ **THE LEARNED LADIES OF PARK AVENUE by David Grimm, translated and freely adapted from Molière's** *Les Femmes Savantes.* Dicky wants to marry Betty, but her mother's plan is for Betty to wed a most pompous man. "A brave, brainy and barmy revision." –*Hartford Courant.* "A rare but welcome bird in contemporary theatre." –*New Haven Register.* "Roll over Cole Porter." –*Boston Globe.* [5M, 5W] ISBN: 978-0-8222-2135-7

★ **REGRETS ONLY by Paul Rudnick.** A sparkling comedy of Manhattan manners that explores the latest topics in marriage, friendships and squandered riches. "One of the funniest quip-meisters on the planet." –*NY Times.* "Precious moments of hilarity. Devastatingly accurate political and social satire." –*BackStage.* "Great fun." –*CurtainUp.* [3M, 3W] ISBN: 978-0-8222-2223-1

DRAMATISTS PLAY SERVICE, INC.
440 Park Avenue South, New York, NY 10016 212-683-8960 Fax 212-213-1539
postmaster@dramatists.com www.dramatists.com

NEW PLAYS

★ **AFTER ASHLEY by Gina Gionfriddo.** A teenager is unwillingly thrust into the national spotlight when a family tragedy becomes talk-show fodder. "A work that virtually any audience would find accessible." –*NY Times.* "Deft characterization and caustic humor." –*NY Sun.* "A smart satirical drama." –*Variety.* [4M, 2W] ISBN: 978-0-8222-2099-2

★ **THE RUBY SUNRISE by Rinne Groff.** Twenty-five years after Ruby struggles to realize her dream of inventing the first television, her daughter faces similar battles of faith as she works to get Ruby's story told on network TV. "Measured and intelligent, optimistic yet clear-eyed." –*NY Magazine.* "Maintains an exciting sense of ingenuity." –*Village Voice.* "Sinuous theatrical flair." –*Broadway.com.* [3M, 4W] ISBN: 978-0-8222-2140-1

★ **MY NAME IS RACHEL CORRIE taken from the writings of Rachel Corrie, edited by Alan Rickman and Katharine Viner.** This solo piece tells the story of Rachel Corrie who was killed in Gaza by an Israeli bulldozer set to demolish a Palestinian home. "Heartbreaking urgency. An invigoratingly detailed portrait of a passionate idealist." –*NY Times.* "Deeply authentically human." –*USA Today.* "A stunning dramatization." –*CurtainUp.* [1W] ISBN: 978-0-8222-2222-4

★ **ALMOST, MAINE by John Cariani.** This charming midwinter night's dream of a play turns romantic clichés on their ear as it chronicles the painfully hilarious amorous adventures (and misadventures) of residents of a remote northern town that doesn't quite exist. "A whimsical approach to the joys and perils of romance." –*NY Times.* "Sweet, poignant and witty." –*NY Daily News.* "Aims for the heart by way of the funny bone." –*Star-Ledger.* [2M, 2W] ISBN: 978-0-8222-2156-2

★ **Mitch Albom's TUESDAYS WITH MORRIE by Jeffrey Hatcher and Mitch Albom, based on the book by Mitch Albom.** The true story of Brandeis University professor Morrie Schwartz and his relationship with his student Mitch Albom. "A touching, life-affirming, deeply emotional drama." –*NY Daily News.* "You'll laugh. You'll cry." –*Variety.* "Moving and powerful." –*NY Post.* [2M] ISBN: 978-0-8222-2188-3

★ **DOG SEES GOD: CONFESSIONS OF A TEENAGE BLOCKHEAD by Bert V. Royal.** An abused pianist and a pyromaniac ex-girlfriend contribute to the teen-angst of America's most hapless kid. "A welcome antidote to the notion that the *Peanuts* gang provides merely American cuteness." –*NY Times.* "Hysterically funny." –*NY Post.* "The *Peanuts* kids have finally come out of their shells." –*Time Out.* [4M, 4W] ISBN: 978-0-8222-2152-4

DRAMATISTS PLAY SERVICE, INC.
440 Park Avenue South, New York, NY 10016   212-683-8960   Fax 212-213-1539
postmaster@dramatists.com   www.dramatists.com

NEW PLAYS

★ **RABBIT HOLE by David Lindsay-Abaire.** Winner of the 2007 Pulitzer Prize. Becca and Howie Corbett have everything a couple could want until a life-shattering accident turns their world upside down. "An intensely emotional examination of grief, laced with wit." –*Variety.* "A transcendent and deeply affecting new play." –*Entertainment Weekly.* "Painstakingly beautiful." –*BackStage.* [2M, 3W] ISBN: 978-0-8222-2154-8

★ **DOUBT, A Parable by John Patrick Shanley.** Winner of the 2005 Pulitzer Prize and Tony Award. Sister Aloysius, a Bronx school principal, takes matters into her own hands when she suspects the young Father Flynn of improper relations with one of the male students. "All the elements come invigoratingly together like clockwork." –*Variety.* "Passionate, exquisite, important, engrossing." –*NY Newsday.* [1M, 3W] ISBN: 978-0-8222-2219-4

★ **THE PILLOWMAN by Martin McDonagh.** In an unnamed totalitarian state, an author of horrific children's stories discovers that someone has been making his stories come true. "A blindingly bright black comedy." –*NY Times.* "McDonagh's least forgiving, bravest play." –*Variety.* "Thoroughly startling and genuinely intimidating." –*Chicago Tribune.* [4M, 5 bit parts (2M, 1W, 1 boy, 1 girl)] ISBN: 978-0-8222-2100-5

★ **GREY GARDENS book by Doug Wright, music by Scott Frankel, lyrics by Michael Korie.** The hilarious and heartbreaking story of Big Edie and Little Edie Bouvier Beale, the eccentric aunt and cousin of Jacqueline Kennedy Onassis, once bright names on the social register who became East Hampton's most notorious recluses. "An experience no passionate theatergoer should miss." –*NY Times.* "A unique and unmissable musical." –*Rolling Stone.* [4M, 3W, 2 girls] ISBN: 978-0-8222-2181-4

★ **THE LITTLE DOG LAUGHED by Douglas Carter Beane.** Mitchell Green could make it big as the hot new leading man in Hollywood if Diane, his agent, could just keep him in the closet. "Devastatingly funny." –*NY Times.* "An out-and-out delight." –*NY Daily News.* "Full of wit and wisdom." –*NY Post.* [2M, 2W] ISBN: 978-0-8222-2226-2

★ **SHINING CITY by Conor McPherson.** A guilt-ridden man reaches out to a therapist after seeing the ghost of his recently deceased wife. "Haunting, inspired and glorious." –*NY Times.* "Simply breathtaking and astonishing." –*Time Out.* "A thoughtful, artful, absorbing new drama." –*Star-Ledger.* [3M, 1W] ISBN: 978-0-8222-2187-6

DRAMATISTS PLAY SERVICE, INC.
440 Park Avenue South, New York, NY 10016 212-683-8960 Fax 212-213-1539
postmaster@dramatists.com www.dramatists.com